THE BRUMBACK LIBRARY
OF VAN WERT COUNTY
VAN WERT, OHIO

IN PROFILE

The First Men Round the World

Andrew Langley

SILVER BURDETT

In Profile

Women of the Air
Founders of Religions
Tyrants of the Twentieth Century
Leaders of the Russian Revolution
Pirates and Privateers
Great Press Barons
Explorers on the Nile
Women Prime Ministers
Founders of America
The Cinema Greats
The War Poets
The First Men Round the World

First published in 1983 by
Wayland Publishers Ltd
49 Lansdowne Place, Hove
East Sussex BN3 1HF, England

© Copyright 1983 Wayland Publishers Ltd

Adapted and Published in the United States by
Silver Burdett Company, Morristown, N.J.

1983 Printing

ISBN 0-382-06640-5

Library of Congress Catalog Card No. 82-61635

Phototypeset by Direct Image, Hove, Sussex
Printed in Italy by G. Canale & C.S.p.A., Turin

Contents

Ferdinand Magellan

Born into the Age of Discovery

Ferdinand Magellan was born in the year 1480, high up in the Portuguese mountain town of Sabrosa. The climate there was harsh, with long, very cold winters and searing hot summers. We know very little about his childhood, except that his father was a nobleman, and that he had three elder sisters and one younger brother.

Magellan's father was able to use his influence to get Ferdinand a position at the Royal Court in Lisbon, as an apprentice at Queen Leonora's School for Pages. The twelve-year-old boy left his remote mountain home, and rarely returned there during the rest of his life.

The pages were supervised by Duke Manuel, the brother-in-law and rival of King John of Portugal. Unfortunately for young Ferdinand, the Duke took an instant dislike to him, and this was to cause him great problems in later life. However, his early years as a page were happy ones. He was taught music, dancing, etiquette, hunting and swordsmanship, as were pages at other courts in Europe. He was also instructed in map-making, astronomy and navigation. King John was very interested in exploring and trading with other parts of the world, and Magellan looked forward to an exciting career at sea.

The port of Lisbon in the sixteenth century.

In 1487, Bartholomew Diaz became the first man to sail round the Cape of Good Hope into the Indian Ocean.

Rivalry with Spain

Certainly, all the talk in Lisbon was about exploration. Recent improvements in navigation techniques meant that ships could sail accurately over far greater distances than ever before, and Portuguese sailors were going further and further in search of trade.

But there was fierce competition from neighbouring Spain. The aim of both Portugal and Spain was to discover a route to the Far East. Beyond the Straits of Malacca (between Malaya and Sumatra) lay China, where beautiful silks could be bought, and the legendary Spice Islands (now known as the Moluccas), where pepper, cloves and nutmegs, highly prized in Europe, were grown.

The first great obstacle was the huge continent of Africa. In 1487, Bartholomew Diaz had sailed round the southernmost tip of Africa in a Portuguese ship, and laid open the way for a new trading route to the Indian Ocean. The Spanish, however, tried to find a route to the Far East by going westwards across the unknown Atlantic, and in 1492 Christopher Columbus became the first European to reach America.

Columbus returned from his heroic voyage in the same year that the young Magellan arrived in Lisbon. The Portuguese were extremely jealous of Spain's success, and rivalry between the two countries grew so intense that Pope Alexander VI was asked to intervene. He fixed an imaginary line around the world from Pole to Pole, dividing the Atlantic in half.

This line, officially agreed upon in the Treaty of Tordesillas in 1494, brought peace for a while. Spain

Christopher Columbus presents an account of his voyage to the King and Queen of Spain.

could explore and trade with all lands to the west of the line, and Portugal was given the lands to the east. This meant that Spain could concentrate on America (except for most of what is now Brazil, which was east of the line), whilst Portugal could explore Africa, the Indian Ocean and beyond.

But, even without Spain, there was plenty of opposition to the Portuguese. The Arabs had controlled all trade with the East for many centuries, and they would have to be defeated before the treasures of China and the Spice Islands could be reached.

Changing fortunes

In 1495, Magellan's ambitions suffered their first great setback—King John was assassinated and Duke Manuel succeeded to the throne. Unlike John, Manuel wanted to concentrate on agriculture rather than exploration, and Magellan's hopes of going to sea seemed to disappear overnight. Although a few expeditions were organized, he stood very little chance of gaining a place on one because he had no influence with the King.

However, one of these Portuguese expeditions was to change things dramatically. In 1498, Vasco da Gama became the first man to sail round the Cape of Good Hope to India. He returned with a fabulous cargo of spices, silks and jewels, and suddenly everyone at Court wanted to sail to India. But still Magellan was overlooked, and he could only watch as sailors returned to Portugal with fame and fortune.

Then, in 1504, Manuel decided to set up a chain of fortified bases along the east coast of Africa and drive the Arabs from the Indian Ocean, and he organized an expedition under Francisco d'Almeida. Excitement mounted as the fleet of twenty-two ships and 2,000 men prepared for the voyage. At last, Magellan got his chance. He gained leave from the Court and enlisted as a seaman.

King Manuel, who came to the Portuguese throne in 1495 after the assassination of King John.

8

Magellan dreams of the Pacific

The fleet set sail in 1505. A series of forts was established along the East African coast, and Magellan was then given the task of patrolling the coast in a small barge armed with six cannon. In fifteen months, he sank more than 200 Arab ships. The power of the Arabs was finally broken by the Portuguese victory off the island of Diu. During the battle, Magellan was so badly wounded that he almost died, and it took him five months to recover.

In 1509, he was aboard the first Portuguese fleet to reach Malacca, one of the greatest trading centres in the East. The Sultan of Malacca welcomed the Portuguese, but he was secretly plotting to kill them. A party of sailors was lured ashore and then attacked. Magellan, who was watching from a boat when the Sultan attacked, quickly rowed ashore and rescued many of the men. For this courageous action he was made an officer.

Two years later he was in the second expedition to Malacca. The Portuguese arrived in force and the Sultan, after suffering several defeats, had no choice but to allow them free passage to the Pacific. The fleet sailed on to the Spice Islands to begin trading, but Magellan headed east towards the Philippines. When he returned to the fleet, he reported that the lands he had discovered could lie to the east of the Tordesillas line—in the Spanish half of the world. He was immediately branded as a troublemaker and sent back to Lisbon in disgrace. King Manuel put him on half-pay and refused him a place on the next expedition to the East. He was out of work and short of money. This was frustrating for Magellan; he was a fine seaman with a reputation for bravery and leadership, and he longed to be in action again. So, in 1513, he volunteered for service in Morocco where the Portuguese were attempting to crush the Moors of North Africa.

For Magellan, it was an ill-fated campaign. During the fighting, he was wounded in the knee—an injury which left him with a limp for the rest of his life. While he was recovering, he was put in charge of the base camp and given the task of distributing the captured prisoners and plunder. But he made enemies, and was unjustly accused of dishonestly trading with the Moors. He immediately returned to Lisbon to protest his innocence to the King. But, by going absent without leave, he simply made matters worse, and Manuel treated him coldly, even after he was found to be not guilty.

Humiliation

The next year was probably the most miserable of Magellan's life. He desperately wanted to get back to the East, but he could not gain command of a ship. Finally, he tried a direct approach to the King, but his request was refused and he was told that there was no place for him in the Portuguese fleet. Humiliated and dejected, Magellan left Lisbon for Porto in the north of the country.

He stayed there for several months, listening to the gossip of the sailors. One of the main topics is sure to have been the discovery of the Pacific Ocean, glimpsed by a Spaniard called Balboa from a hilltop in Central America. Soon, a plan began to form in Magellan's mind: if a ship could somehow get into this new ocean, it might reach the Philippines and the Spice Islands by sailing westward rather than eastward.

But there were two great problems to be solved. Firstly, how could a ship get round America? This was answered by John of Lisbon, himself a great navigator and seaman, and a good friend of Magellan's. He believed he had discovered a narrow strait, far to the south, which gave free passage into the Pacific and was sheltered from the dreadful storms of the area.

The other problem was less easy to solve. A voyage across the Atlantic would take Magellan into seas which the Treaty of Tordesillas had allotted to Spain,

A fleet of carracks sets sail. It was in ships like these that the Portuguese embarked upon their expeditions to the East.

and would lay him open to attacks by Spanish ships. He had almost certainly thought about leaving Portugal after his rejection by King Manuel. His mind was finally made up when he received an unexpected visit from Duarte Barbosa, an old friend who, like Magellan, had returned to Lisbon to face a cool reception from Manuel. He had crossed over to Spain to join an influential relative, and together they had hit upon the idea of organizing a private expedition to the Spice Islands via John of Lisbon's strait. Barbosa had come to Porto to ask Magellan to command their expedition.

Across the border

So, in 1517, Magellan made his momentous decision and crossed the border to Seville in Spain. He was joined later by Ruy de Faleira, a brilliant but unstable astronomer who had taught him much about the stars and their use in navigation, with the result that

11

Magellan pleaded with King Manuel to be given command of a ship sailing to the East, but his appeal was rejected.

Magellan was probably the most accurate navigator of his age.

Unfortunately, Barbosa was unable to finance the expedition himself, and so Magellan was introduced to three men who agreed to provide a lot of the necessary money. These men—Juan de Aranda, Bishop Fonseca and Cristobal de Haro—were interested solely in finding a quick route to the Spice Islands, whereas Magellan's aim was to reach the Philippines. This conflict of interests was to cause great problems during the voyage.

In the meantime, however, Magellan presented his plans to the young King Charles of Spain. Charles was, at first, suspicious of the weather-beaten, tough-looking Portuguese sailor, but he was quick to see the importance of the voyage, and he agreed to it then and there. Magellan was knighted and made captain-general of the expedition, with orders to sail first to the Spice Islands, and then to the Philippines to claim them for Spain.

Too late, King Manuel learnt of the voyage and realized what he had let slip through his hands. He protested angrily to King Charles, but he was ignored. He also sent spies to report on the preparations and cause as much mischief as they could. At the same time, the Spanish financiers, anxious to make sure that the voyage was simply a profitable trading venture to the Spice Islands, were trying to undermine Magellan's authority. They managed to get their own men appointed to many of the key positions in the fleet —three of the five captains were chosen by them—and by the time the expedition was ready to leave, more than half of the officers were plotting to kill Magellan and seize command.

King Charles I of Spain.

The great voyage

At last, in 1519, the small fleet set out. Magellan's flagship was the *Trinidad*, and behind him in close formation were the *San Antonio*, the *Concepcion*, the *Victoria* and the *Santiago*.

They made good progress, and reached the Canary Islands in six days. Even as early as this, Magellan was warned that a mutiny was planned, but he took no hasty action. The ringleader, one of the captains appointed by the financiers of the expedition, eventually went too far in his attempts to provoke a confrontation with Magellan. He was immediately locked up. Magellan had retained command, but there was worse to come.

The five ships reached Brazil and, after a pleasant stay in Rio de Janeiro, they began to make their way down the South American coast, searching for the strait which would take them into the Pacific.

Mutiny!

Suddenly, on 11th January 1520, they rounded a south-facing headland and found a broad stretch of water. Magellan was jubilant, and he sent the *Santiago* to explore. She returned a few days later with bad news: John of Lisbon's strait was not a passage to the Pacific, but the mouth of a large river (the Rio de la Plata). This was a bitter blow for Magellan; so much so that at first he refused to believe it. Eventually, however, he was convinced, and he began searching further south, despite mounting opposition from both the officers and the crew.

Winter was setting in, and he decided to shelter from the weather for a few months in the Bay of St Julian. When the men landed, he ordered them to build huts on the bleak, inhospitable shore, and, since food was running low, he cut the daily rations.

This was the last straw for some of the men, who wanted to sail for home. Shortly after Easter Day, the

Magellan and his crew were greeted enthusiastically by the natives of Rio de Janeiro.

This map, drawn after Magellan's voyage, shows the Rio de la Plata (near the top) and the Straits of Magellan.

San Antonio was boarded by mutineers from the *Victoria* and the *Concepcion*. Magellan was in a desperate position, with only his flagship and the smaller *Santiago* under his control. But, once again, he did not rush into action. When night fell, he sent a party to offer terms to the mutinous captain of the *Victoria*. When these were refused, the captain was killed and the ship recaptured. Two days later, the *San Antonio* drifted from her moorings, and Magellan boarded her in the confusion. The captain of the remaining ship knew he was beaten, and surrendered.

The forty mutineers were swiftly tried and condemned to death, although Magellan eventually let most of them off, executing only one of the ringleaders and marooning two others. But, as winter continued, rebellion was still in the air.

But everything else was soon forgotten when a greater disaster overtook the expedition. Magellan sent the *Santiago* to explore the coast further south, in the hope of finding a better area for hunting and fishing. The ship was caught in a furious storm and driven on to the rocks. The crew managed to scramble ashore, and two brave men made the harrowing walk back through the jungle (and across a huge river) to get help from Magellan. Eventually all the men were rescued.

Spring came at last, and the four remaining ships set off again, probing along the coastline. After several disappointments, they turned into an inlet which seemed much wider and longer than the others they had tried. With mounting excitement, they pushed on until the channel divided into two. Magellan's flagship and the *Victoria* searched one way, while the other two ships were sent the other.

Magellan soon found that his channel was the correct one, and he turned back to wait for the others to join him. But only the *Concepcion* arrived, and her captain said that he had lost touch with the *San Antonio*.

Magellan had no way of knowing that the largest ship in his fleet, with valuable provisions and men on board, had once again been taken over by mutineers, and had turned to sail back to Spain.

Into the unknown

He was now down to three ships and running low on food, but he pushed on. Just before Christmas 1520, they joyfully reached the Pacific Ocean, and set sail across this unknown stretch of sea. But they had no idea of the vastness of the Pacific, and their joy evaporated as the weeks passed. Finally, the food ran out, the water became undrinkable, and the crew were attacked by scurvy. They got so hungry that all the rats in the bilges were eaten, and even the leather from the rigging was torn down and stewed. Nineteen men died during that terrible crossing. Finally, after ninety-eight days, they sighted the group of islands now known as the Marianas. The natives were far

Magellan discovers the channel leading to the Pacific Ocean.

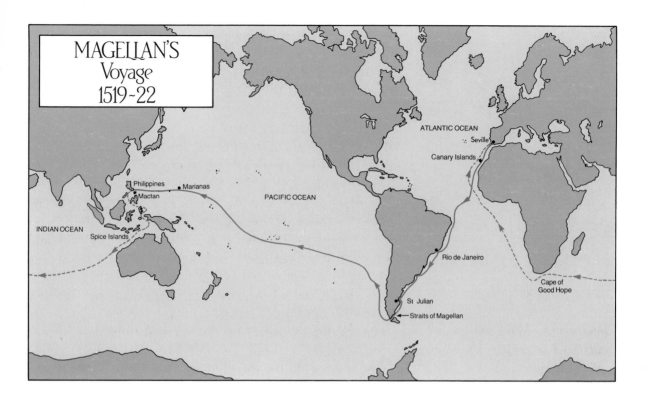

The route taken by the Victoria on her round-the-world voyage. The dotted line shows the course by which Sebastian del Cano returned from the Philippines to Spain.

from friendly: they boarded the *Trinidad* and looted whatever they could carry while the crew, still weak from hunger and sickness, were forced to look on. Only when Magellan ordered his crossbowmen to open fire did the attackers retreat. The sailors had to launch a landing party in order to steal the food and water they needed so desperately.

The little fleet soon sailed on towards the Philippines, where they were warmly received by the local chieftain. Tribesmen were invited on board, and were greatly impressed when Magellan fired his cannon for them. Magellan was overjoyed—he had reached his goal at last. His officers and crew were also happy for the time being since the Philippines, although some way north of the Spice Islands, were rich in gold and spices. Magellan claimed the islands for Spain and made trading agreements.

The fleet stayed for many months at the island of

Magellan's attack on the island of Mactan.

Unable to escape, Magellan was killed by the natives.

Cebu, where a market was set up, and the local ruler, the Rajah, was converted to Christianity. Soon the whole island followed his example, and came to look upon the small and determined white man as a saint.

A tragic end

Magellan became convinced that he was not only an explorer, but a crusader and missionary as well. Unfortunately, his religious zeal seems to have overcome his good sense. When he was told that the chieftain of the neighbouring island of Mactan had refused to become a Christian, he organized a raiding party to punish him. So blinded was he by his religious fervour that he made his first, and only, mistake in the whole expedition.

Refusing the help of more than a thousand Cebu warriors, he landed on Mactan with only sixty Spaniards. He put his trust in God, and in his own weapons and armour. The attack was a disaster. On landing, they were immediately attacked by a huge army of natives and driven from the beach into the sea. Magellan, slowed down by his limp, was quickly overtaken and hacked to death.

Throughout the entire ill-fated attack, the Spanish captains looked on, refusing the King of Cebu's pleas to go to Magellan's aid. They wanted to press on to the Spice Islands—the whole object of the voyage as far as they were concerned—and they saw Magellan and his attempts to convert the Philippines to Christianity as hindrances to their plans. Only when it was clear that their captain-general was dead did they move in to pick up survivors, and they did not even bother to rescue his body from the sea.

It was a tragic and wasteful end to a great adventure. With the death of Magellan, the influence of Spain and Christianity in the Philippines evaporated overnight. The markets were broken up, and the King of Cebu, who had become a good friend of

The Victoria, *the only ship of Magellan's fleet to complete the first circumnavigation of the world.*

Magellan's, lured thirty Spanish officers ashore and murdered them. The rest fled to Borneo, abandoning the leaky *Concepcion* on the way, and destroying Magellan's papers in an attempt to cover the tracks of their treachery. The expedition had turned into a shambles, although it did manage to reach the Spice Islands, where the two remaining ships loaded up with a valuable cargo of spices, silks and gold.

When they came to return home, the *Trinidad* was left behind—she was so overladen that she ran aground and was captured by the Portuguese. Only the *Victoria* remained. Her captain, strangely enough, was one of the men who had mutinied at Port St Julian —Sebastian del Cano. Under his leadership, the *Victoria* crossed the Indian Ocean and rounded the Cape of Good Hope, reaching Seville late in 1522. Only eighteen men out of 277 had lived to complete the first circumnavigation of the world.

Dates and events

1480   Ferdinand Magellan born in Sabrosa, Portugal.

1492   Becomes an apprentice at Queen Leonora's School for Pages in Lisbon.

1494   Treaty of Tordesillas divides the world in half, between Portugal and Spain.

1505   Magellan goes to sea for the first time, with Francisco d'Almeida's expedition to the Indian Ocean.

1512   Magellan discovers the Philippines, suggests they might lie in Spain's half of the world, and is sent back to Portugal in disgrace.

1513   Volunteers for service against the Moors in Morocco.

1514   Is accused of dishonesty, and returns to Lisbon to protest his innocence.

1516   Appeals to King Manuel of Portugal to be given command of an expedition to the East, but is rejected.

1517   Crosses the border to Spain, and presents his plan for a voyage to the Pacific to King Charles.

1519   Fleet of five ships and 227 men set sail from Seville in Spain.

1520   Magellan crushes mutiny at Port St Julian. Fleet enters the Pacific Ocean.

1521   Ships reach the Philippines. Magellan is killed on the island of Mactan.

1522   One ship and eighteen men return to Seville—completion of the first circumnavigation of the world.

Francis Drake

From slave-trader to buccaneer

Although he is always thought of as a Devon man, Francis Drake spent little of his childhood in that county. He was born in about the year 1540, and brought up by his father to hold strong Protestant views. But the south-west of England was, at that time, a fervently Catholic area, and it was not long before the Drakes (and many other families) were forced to flee in the face of violent hostility.

They moved to Kent, and lived a precarious life on board one of the old navy 'hulks' moored in the River Medway near Chatham. Drake's father was appointed chaplain to the sailors there. Thus, Francis Drake grew up with two great passions in his heart—a love for ships and the sea, and a hatred for the Catholics who had driven him from his home. They were to make him the greatest sailor and most feared buccaneer of his age.

Drake gained his first experience of sailing when he became an apprentice on a small trading boat which carried goods between the River Thames and Holland. In an age when navigation was very much a hit-and-miss affair, the Thames estuary was a treacherous place in which to sail, and the young Drake learned his skills the hard way. But he must have done well, for when his employer died he left his boat to him. Drake continued trading for a while, but he was dreaming of adventure on a much grander scale.

He was lucky to have influential relations in Plymouth—the rich and successful Hawkins family. At this time, William and John Hawkins were busy building up the slave trade, capturing or buying natives on the west coast of Africa and shipping them to the West Indies, where they were sold as cheap labour to the Spanish colonists. To us this seems a vile trade, but it was an acceptable and highly profitable one to the merchants of the time, and Drake was eager to take part.

In 1566, he sold his trading boat and made his first trip with the Hawkins' fleet across the Atlantic. The next year, he was given his first ship to command during another voyage. But it was to be an unpleasant experience. John Hawkins' flagship was forced to put in for repairs at the port of San Juan de Ulua on the Spanish Main. Although there was a large Spanish fleet in the harbour, the English were granted safe conduct (there was no official war between the two nations at this time). Hostages were exchanged, and Hawkins seized the gun battery at the harbour mouth as a safeguard.

Ships like this Elizabethan man-o-war were a familiar sight to the young Francis Drake when his family moved to Chatham.

Sir John Hawkins, who introduced Drake to slave-trading.

Spanish treachery

Suddenly the Spaniards attacked, and their fireships bore down on the English fleet. Hawkins quickly ordered a retreat, which Drake obeyed immediately, sailing his ship, the *Judith*, back to England without stopping to offer help. As it was, only one other ship, the *Minion*, managed to escape, and this was so desperately overcrowded that over a hundred men had to be put ashore on the Mexican coast, where most were captured and killed by Spaniards. Eventually the *Minion* reached England with only fifteen men left alive.

This strange and tragic episode had two consequences for Drake. First of all, it fired him with a hatred of all Spaniards, whom he now saw as treacherous and callous: in the years to come, they were to suffer for it. Then there was the puzzling matter of Drake's flight from the scene of battle.

23

The Spanish Empire in the Caribbean. Drake planned to attack the ports and shipping in the West Indies and along the north coast of South America.

Although Hawkins later forgave him, he wrote in his journal at the time that his cousin 'forsook us in our great misery'. Perhaps Drake's eagerness for revenge was increased by a feeling of guilt for his action.

Although thirsting to get back at his enemies, Drake lay low for the next four years. In fact, he was preparing the ground. Apart from his gifts as a leader, as a navigator and as a fighter, his future successes were mostly to be based on careful planning.

Drake's aim was to attack the Spanish ports and shipping in the West Indies and the Spanish Main, thereby disrupting the Spanish navy and plundering some of the fabulous treasures that were annually transported from South America to Europe. His first step had been to find a safe harbour on the Panama Coast from which to launch his attacks. He had discovered the perfect place—a secret inlet which he named Port Pheasant. It was then unknown to the Spaniards and was well stocked with fish and game, and Drake had soon made friends with the local Indians, the Cimarrons.

Thus prepared, he set out from Plymouth in 1572 with two ships, the *Pasco* and the *Swan*, both heavily armed. But a shock awaited him at Port Pheasant—he found the smouldering remains of a fire, and a lead plate nailed to a tree. On the plate was scratched a message from another buccaneer, John Garret, telling him that the Spaniards had found his hideaway, and warning him to leave at once.

Drake's reaction was typical. He immediately set out to attack before the Spaniards knew he was in the area. Not far to the north-west lay the town of Nombre de Dios, where the Spaniards loaded their gold and silver on to ships to transport it back to Spain. At three in the morning, Drake's ships crept into the harbour to attack the town. But the alarm was sounded and the attack failed. Drake, wounded in the leg, was forced to order the retreat.

Drake catches his first sight of the Pacific Ocean.

A glimpse of the Pacific

When he had recovered, he decided to raid the mule-train which brought the Spanish treasure from Panama to Nombre de Dios, and so he headed inland towards the mountains. It was then that he was inspired with a quite different dream. On reaching the summit of a ridge, the Cimarrons showed Drake a tall tree with a platform built in it. Climbing up, he saw the distant sparkle of the Pacific Ocean, the first Englishman to do so. Then and there he vowed that he would one day 'sail an English ship in those seas'.

After one failed attempt, a mule-train was successfully plundered with the aid of a French pirate. The raiders staggered away with as much gold and silver as they could carry, burying the rest for a return visit. To add insult to injury, Drake stole two Spanish ships to carry the treasure home in (he had previously sunk his own to avoid making his presence known). Three weeks later they arrived back in Plymouth, where the citizens abandoned their church services to rush out and welcome them.

Drake's voyage round the world

Drake's sensational success was very popular in England, where hatred of Spain was growing rapidly. But since the two countries were not at war, Queen Elizabeth could not congratulate him openly. So he was sent to guard the coast of Ireland for some years until the excitement died down. During this dull assignment, he met Thomas Doughty, a man with friends at Court, and the two discussed Drake's dream of sailing to the Pacific.

Meanwhile, the Queen and some of the members of her Court were devising a plan to send an expedition to the Spice Islands. This had to be kept secret in case the Portuguese (who controlled all trade with the Spice Islands) heard of the venture. It was announced that the purpose of the voyage was to find out whether South America was a continuous piece of land stretching far into the south, perhaps joined to a legendary, undiscovered continent called *Terra Australis*.

Drake was appointed to lead the expedition. His orders were to reach the Spice Islands and return with a profitable cargo. But he was sure that those who had put up the money for the voyage, including the Queen herself, would not mind *how* he carried out these orders, and he looked forward to continuing his own holy war against the Catholic Spaniards by plundering their settlements on the west coast of America.

It was with this mixture of aims, public and secret, that the small fleet set out from Plymouth in September 1577. Drake, now a captain-general, led in the *Pelican*, followed by four other ships, the *Elizabeth*, the *Marigold*, the *Swan*, and a small supply-ship, the *Christopher*. Among the crew was Drake's friend Thomas Doughty.

Despite a bad storm, all went well at first. Off the Cape Verde Islands, Drake captured some Portuguese ships, on board one of which he found an experienced pilot who could guide him to the Pacific. As he had no charts or maps, this was a lucky find. The fleet then crossed the Atlantic to Port St Julian, where they

Queen Elizabeth I.

Thomas Doughty was tried and beheaded at Port St Julian.

found a grim reminder of Magellan's voyage—the gibbet on which the ringleader of the mutiny had been hanged.

Doughty beheaded

As on Magellan's voyage, mutiny broke out at Port St Julian. Doughty, unused to being commanded by others, would not take Drake's orders seriously, and he was charged with trying to discredit the Captain-General. He was also accused of witchcraft—it was said that he was responsible for the unfavourable winds and storms they had encountered. After a short 'trial', Doughty was beheaded.

By prompt and savage action, Drake had restored complete order. To finish the affair, he chose to speak to his men when they were assembled for the next Sunday Service. He exhorted them to stick together, and ordered the 'gentlemen' on board to work side by side with the common sailors. If any wished to go home, he said, they could have the *Marigold* to sail in. No one spoke.

With his band united again, and the flagship re-named the *Golden Hind*, Drake set sail for the Straits of Magellan. His ship passed through the Straits in half the time that Magellan had taken, but was the only one to make it. The *Swan* had already been abandoned, and now the *Marigold* sank in a storm with all hands, and the crew of the *Elizabeth* had forced their captain to turn back and sail for Plymouth. Undeterred, Drake pushed on to make his first important discovery, the channel between Tierra del Fuego and Antarctica, which is still known as Drake's Passage. It was clear that if *Terra Australis* did exist, it was not joined to South America.

He then headed north along the coasts of Chile and Peru. This was the easiest and most dazzling programme of plunder that any English sailor had ever embarked upon. The Spaniards themselves had stolen the fabulous treasures of gold, silver and jewels from

A sixteenth-century Spanish galleon.

When Drake landed in 'New Albion' he was crowned by the local Indians, who thought he was a god.

the South American Indians. But because no other Europeans ever sailed into the Pacific, they felt safe from attack and left their settlements undefended. However, they had reckoned without the boldness of the stocky, blond-haired Englishman.

Starting at Valparaiso, where he captured a treasure ship virtually unopposed, Drake blazed his way up the coast. The settlements had so little protection that he rarely needed to use force, once taking 4,000 ducats from a Spaniard as he slept! His richest prize of all was the galleon *Spitfire*, which was captured without loss of life, and which was laden, not only with gold bars, unminted silver and chests of jewels, but also with plenty of fresh food.

The most famous man in the land

Now packed with enough treasure to pay for the trip many times over, the *Golden Hind* sailed north as far as present-day San Francisco. Drake named the land 'New Albion' and claimed it for Queen Elizabeth. Then he headed westward across the broad ocean to the Spice Islands. Here, the Sultan greeted him enthusiastically. He had just quarrelled with the Portuguese and was glad to agree to a treaty with England—in return for the help of Queen Elizabeth's navy, he offered to grant English merchants a monopoly of his spice trade.

Somehow, room was found for six tonnes of cloves, and Drake began the long voyage home. The journey, across the Indian Ocean and round the Cape of Good Hope, was uneventful, except for one terrifying moment when the *Golden Hind* got stuck on a coral reef. By throwing out half the guns, half the fresh water and half the cloves, the ship was lightened just enough to clear the reef.

Drake made his second triumphant return to Plymouth in the autumn of 1580—the first man to have led an expedition right round the world. The treasure he had captured was worth about

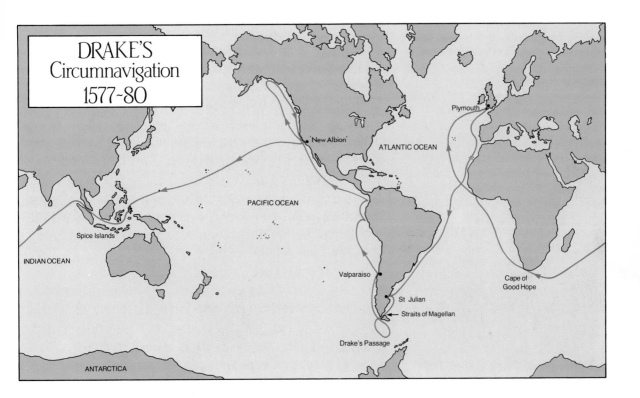

DRAKE'S
Circumnavigation
1577~80

Plymouth

'New Albion'

ATLANTIC OCEAN

PACIFIC OCEAN

Spice Islands

INDIAN OCEAN

Valparaiso

St Julian

Straits of Magellan

Cape of
Good Hope

Drake's Passage

ANTARCTICA

The route taken by Francis Drake in the Golden Hind.

£13,000,000 ($24,000,000) in today's money, and he had shown how vulnerable the Spanish Pacific empire was. In April 1581, Queen Elizabeth went aboard the *Golden Hind* at Deptford, London, and knighted her commander—Drake's circumnavigation of the world, and his humiliation of the Spaniards, was officially rewarded. He was the most famous man in the land.

In recognition of his voyage, Drake was knighted by Queen Elizabeth aboard the Golden Hind.

The defeat of the Spanish Armada, and Drake's last days

Drake bought himself a fine house, Buckland Abbey, near Plymouth, and became Mayor of Plymouth, and its Member of Parliament. But as the friction between England and Spain flamed into open warfare, and England was threatened with invasion, his leadership and courage were soon needed again.

By 1585, he was eager to get back into the fray, and the Queen asked him to start unofficial raids on Spanish shipping, to punish Philip II for seizing English trading vessels. Drake was given a larger fleet than ever before—twenty-one ships and 2,300 men—and he set out to terrorize the Spanish colonies in the West Indies.

The first target was the wealthy town of Santo Domingo. Attacking by land and sea, he took the town easily and forced a huge ransom from the governor. A few months later, his brilliant tactics toppled the defences of an even richer town—Cartagena—and this time the ransom was even larger.

Not waiting for Spanish reprisals, and fearing the yellow fever that raged in the area, Drake now performed his second task. This was to take supplies to the new English colony of Virginia, and at the port of Roanoke he took on board many of the settlers who wanted to go home. Once again, his voyage had been gloriously successful. His buccaneering exploits had caused panic in the Spanish Empire, and caused Philip to use much-needed wealth for the building of new defences. Even more important, he had shown that England had a navy to be reckoned with.

In 1587, Drake achieved the most daring of all his successes—a breath-taking dash into the heart of the Spanish navy anchored in Cadiz harbour. The port was full of Spanish ships, gathering for an invasion of England, and Drake sailed straight into the inner harbour, using his customary weapon of surprise. All was bedlam, and he was able to sink thirty-two ships, including the Spanish Admiral's flagship, and sail away with four Spanish ships and plenty of loot.

Buckland Abbey—the house which Drake bought after returning from his great voyage round the world.

Drake afterwards described this as 'singeing the King of Spain's beard'. Although he had not really delayed the planned invasion of England by King Philip, he had shown what havoc the smaller and nimbler English ships could cause. But even he could not hold back the sailing of the enormous Armada, which arrived off the coast of Cornwall in the summer of 1588. This huge fleet of 130 ships was heading for Calais, where it was to take on board the invasion force of 30,000 troops.

This was to be Drake's greatest hour. With his commander, Lord Howard, he led a hundred English ships in a chase all along the English Channel. Before the Armada could pick up the soldiers at Calais, Howard sent in fireships which broke up their careful formation. Scattered and pinned to the coast, the

This letter from Queen Elizabeth I to Drake was written just before his daring attack on the Spanish fleet in Cadiz harbour. It gives him full power to deal with any disobedience among the crew.

The Battle of the Spanish Armada. When the Spanish fleet was pinned to the coast, the English sent in fireships.

One of Drake's men at the time of the Armada.

Spanish ships were easy prey for Drake and his marauding colleagues.

The final disaster for the Spaniards was a sudden change of wind, which blew them northward into the North Sea and then west around the treacherous coasts of Scotland and Ireland. The dreadful seas took an even heavier toll than the English fleet, and only about eighty ships struggled back to Seville, many of them barely afloat.

Drake's luck turns

The defeat of the Armada marked the end of Drake's incredible run of successes, for his last two expeditions were sad failures. In 1589, he persuaded the Queen to follow up the defeat of the Armada by attacking the combined kingdoms of Spain and Portugal and capturing Lisbon. Despite the huge fleet and powerful army that he was granted, the voyage was a shambles and half the men died, mostly of disease. Drake was not employed again for five years.

Then, in 1595, Queen Elizabeth heard that the power of Spain was growing again, and a new armada was being built. Drake and John Hawkins persuaded her to attack the Spanish in the Caribbean. But the lessons of the past had been learned—the Spaniards

Drake died of yellow fever and was buried at sea.

now guarded their harbours with huge gun batteries and escorted their treasure fleets with fast ships. Despite minor successes, the English ships inflicted little damage upon their enemies.

Early in 1596, Sir Francis Drake caught the yellow fever that was raging on the Spanish Main. He died on 27th January and was buried at sea—a fitting grave for one of the greatest of all seamen.

Dates and events

James Cook

Catching up after a late start

James Cook was born in 1728, and he spent his childhood in the Yorkshire village of Marton. His father, a farm labourer, was determined that his son should better himself by learning a safe and steady trade. As the young James was good with figures, he was sent to learn shopkeeping in the tiny fishing village of Staithes.

But a dull life behind a counter was not for James Cook. He soon fell in love with the sea, and gave his father no rest until he allowed him to become an apprentice seaman. At eighteen, he was rather old— apprentices usually started at about thirteen—and he had a lot of catching up to do.

His first job was aboard a trading ship carrying coal from the port of Whitby down to London, or across the North Sea to Norway. Like Francis Drake before him, he found that this was a tough training ground for a young sailor, full of treacherous sandbanks, and prone to sudden storms. In those days there were no light-ships and few marker buoys or accurate charts.

For nine years, Cook worked hard and learned the rudiments of seamanship. He rose from apprentice to the rank of mate, and would almost certainly have soon been given his first command. But his sights were set on something higher, and he decided to volunteer for the Royal Navy. It was a courageous and

The small cottage in Marton, Yorkshire, where Cook was born in 1728.

unusual step—conditions aboard naval ships were horrific at that time, and most sailors had to be press-ganged. What is more, it was likely that Cook might never have the chance to command a ship, because few men rose out of the ranks.

It was not long, however, before his superior officers realized that they had a remarkable man on their hands. Cook was a tall, imposing figure, with a strong face and a steady gaze. Everything he did was performed with skill, efficiency and attention to detail, and he was eager to learn at every opportunity. His progress towards fame went on its quiet but steady way—from able seaman, he was promoted to petty officer, and then to master.

In 1758, Cook at last had a chance to show what a superb seaman he was. As master of the 64-gun sloop *Pembroke*, he crossed the Atlantic for the first time, part of a large fleet whose mission was to defeat the French in Canada. At the heart of the expedition was a plan to attack the city of Quebec, the key to the vital St Lawrence River.

The capture of Quebec

The French had removed all the buoys and other markers from the mouth of the river, making it impossible for the big English ships to find a safe passage. The task of re-charting this treacherous stretch of water and replacing the marker buoys fell to James Cook of the *Pembroke*. He did the job extremely well, so well that not one vessel was grounded as the fleet made its silent way upriver to capture Quebec.

It was clear that Cook was an outstanding pilot and navigator. In 1762, he was commissioned to chart the coastline of Newfoundland, with its storms, fogs and deadly icebergs. He stuck to it for the next five years, using all his spare time to learn more about the sciences of surveying, astronomy and mathematics, and he was eventually given his first command. Gradually, the uneducated farm labourer's son was turning himself into the most thoughtful and efficient sailor of his time.

A map of the St Lawrence River showing the English ships attacking the city of Quebec.

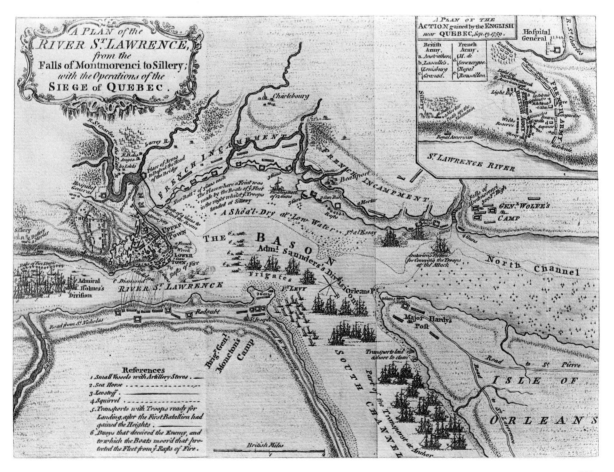

In search of the unknown continent

In 1768, Cook was promoted to lieutenant and appointed to command H.M.S. *Endeavour* on a long voyage into the Pacific. His official mission was to set up an observatory on the island of Tahiti, from which the planet Venus could be seen as it passed across the face of the sun—this only happened every hundred years, and precise observation of it would be of great value to astronomers. The Royal Society had asked King George III for funds for the expedition, and he had agreed, partly because there was a more sensational reason for the voyage, kept secret until Cook had sailed. He was to look for a huge, unknown continent, called *Terra Australis*, which was thought to exist in the southern hemisphere. Drake, in his circumnavigation, had shown that there was no such continent joined to South America. Australia (not to be confused with *Terra Australis*) had been sighted, but was not considered big enough to be the 'missing' continent.

No one had yet been able to explore the Pacific Ocean thoroughly enough to find this continent, if it existed. They were deterred by the huge area to be searched—nearly a third of the Earth's surface—and by the murderous sailing conditions in the southern latitudes. The typhoons, complex currents, fogs and ice were too much for many sailing ships to cope with.

On 26th August 1768, the little *Endeavour* set off from Plymouth. She was a Whitby collier of the type that Cook had sailed in his early days at sea, squarely built and with a very shallow draught. Completely refitted, she carried a crew of seventy, plus a band of scientists, observers and botanists, including Joseph Banks, who was later to become President of the Royal Society, and Daniel Solander.

After stopping at Madeira to take on 3,000 gallons of wine, the ship crossed the Atlantic and rounded the dreaded Cape Horn with little trouble. Cook then headed north-west towards Tahiti.

A model of H.M.S. Endeavour.

Funchal, the capital of Madeira.

Already some of his unique qualities as a leader were obvious. No one was suffering from scurvy—a terrible disease which could destroy a whole crew—because he insisted that every man should eat fresh vegetables or fruit every day. He also made sure that the rest of their food was better than the usual rotten horsemeat and wormy ship's biscuit dished out on most other ships at the time. The cramped sleeping quarters were regularly cleaned and aired, and Cook even provided all hands with fishing rods to ensure a constant supply of fresh fish. Such care for health was unheard of in the Navy, but the result was that the *Endeavour's* crew was fit and happy.

They arrived at Tahiti well in advance of the passage of Venus, and Cook used the time to make an accurate survey of the island. They were greeted joyfully by the natives, and the island itself, with its

A ceremonial dance on Tahiti.

Joseph Banks.

dramatic scenery and happy atmosphere, was like a paradise. But, once the observatory had been built and the course of Venus had been noted, Cook and his crew reluctantly had to leave.

Attacked by cannibals

They sailed southward in search of *Terra Australis*, but they found no trace of the mysterious continent and headed westward. On 7th October 1769, Cook sighted the North Island of New Zealand, where no white man had ever landed. But he found no welcome: the bloodthirsty Maoris were cannibals, and they swarmed out in their war canoes to attack the ship. Only the sailors' muskets drove them back, and Cook was forced to sail further south to look for water and food. Once refreshed, he sailed around the coastlines of both North and South Islands, discovering Cook Strait and making accurate charts. He also took possession of the whole country for King George III.

Even after this long and difficult voyage, the *Endeavour* was still in good repair, and the crew, thanks to Cook's strict diet, were healthy and cheerful. There was nothing to stop him from turning straight round and going home, but after discussion with his officers he decided to continue and explore the coast of Australia, then known as 'New Holland'.

Although the Dutch had discovered Tasmania and sighted the wild west coast of Australia, they had never found the friendlier east coast. Cook, sailing westward, sighted the south-east tip of the huge land mass—now called Cape Howe. He then turned north-ward along the coast, and made his first landfall at Botany Bay, so called because of the large number of plants Banks and Solander collected here. The scientists were also thrilled by the exciting new animals they found—including, of course, the kangaroo. During the voyage, they collected 1,300 new plant and animal species.

After her hull was damaged on a coral reef, the Endeavour *was beached for repair on the east coast of Australia.*

Cook takes possession of Australia for King George III.

Stuck on the Reef

As the *Endeavour* continued northward, she entered a region even more perilous than Cape Horn itself—the Great Barrier Reef. Huge teeth of jagged coral, often hidden just below the waves, threatened the ship at every moment. Navigation was a nightmare. Then, one night, there was a terrifying tearing sound, and the ship was stuck fast on the coral. Rowing boats could not pull her off, and water began to pour into the hold. Eventually, after throwing some guns and other weight overboard, she was hauled off at high tide into deeper water. When she was beached for repair, it was found that the worst hole had been plugged by a broken piece of coral. Without this piece of luck, the *Endeavour* would certainly have sunk.

Once out of the Reef, and having claimed the whole territory of Australia for the King, Cook made for Java, where he wanted to rest and take on supplies. But in the Dutch colony of Batavia tragedy struck. After losing only eight men on the long and dangerous voyage (none of them through sickness), the crew fell prey to the malaria and dysentery that were raging in the port. Cook put to sea again as soon as possible, but by the time he reached home again in 1771, there were only fifty-six survivors.

A mixed reception, and another voyage

In spite of all Cook's achievements, the voyage was not looked upon as a complete success. No great southern continent had been found, and Cook's observations of Venus proved to be rather inaccurate —although this was no fault of his. Banks and Solander, with their flora and fauna, enjoyed most of the glory. Cook's only reward was promotion to commander.

However, he was appointed to lead a second expedition to explore the Pacific as far south as possible. The bold aim of this was to sail completely round the South Pole, as near as the ice would permit. In this way, if *Terra Australis* did exist, it could not be missed. Cook was given two new Whitby colliers, the *Resolution* and the *Adventure*.

Thus, only a year after his return, he left Plymouth again and headed for the Antarctic by way of the Cape of Good Hope. He planned to explore the South Pacific in three segments—one each year, with a period of refitting and relaxation in the warmer seas further north. On board, he had a valuable new aid to navigation, an accurate chronometer which would enable him to work out his longitude.

Into the ice

From the Cape the two ships headed due south and, early in 1773, became the first European vessels to cross the Antarctic Circle. The conditions there were more hellish than any the seaman had ever known, with icy winds that froze their hands to the rigging, pack ice that threatened to crush the hulls, and treacherous icebergs lurking beneath the waves. All around them the gales shrieked and the shifting ice groaned and thundered.

When the ice finally stopped him, Cook turned away from those inhospitable waters and set sail for New Zealand. He had lost touch with the *Adventure*, but found her again at his favourite anchorage, Queen Charlotte Sound. He was shocked to find that his strict measures to prevent scurvy were being ignored, and several of the *Adventure*'s crew were ill. Quickly, boat-loads of greenstuff were harvested, and health and discipline returned.

Then the second part of the voyage began. After paying another visit to Tahiti, Cook sailed on to the Tongan Islands. He renamed them the Friendly Islands, because of the warm reception he was given by the inhabitants. Then, on the way back to Queen Charlotte Sound, Cook again lost contact with the *Adventure* in a storm. Her captain, Tobias Furneaux, eventually decided to return to England by way of the southern oceans, thus becoming the first commander to sail his ship around the world from west to east.

The end of the search

Cook, meanwhile, was heading for the South Pole on the last leg of his search. He zigzagged across the remaining unexplored area of the South Pacific,

The Resolution *and the* Adventure *at anchor in the harbour of the beautiful island of Tahiti.*

Table Bay, near the Cape of Good Hope.

re-crossing the Antarctic Circle and reaching the latitude of 71° 10' South, the furthest south anyone had ever been. Here, the ice formed a solid barrier, and the *Resolution* was forced to turn back. But by now, Cook was convinced that there could be no such continent as *Terra Australis*, unless it was hidden beneath the Antarctic ice.

He then returned to Tahiti, visiting Easter Island and the Marquesas Islands on the way. After exploring Fiji and the New Hebrides, he decided to head for home via New Zealand, and he reached Plymouth in July 1775.

He had sailed over 120,000 miles (195,000 kilometres) and proved that there was no *Terra Australis*; he had sailed further south than any other man; he had accurately charted the South Pacific for the first time; his ships were the first to circumnavigate the world in an easterly direction; and, in all this time, he had not lost a single man through scurvy.

At last, he was properly rewarded for these astonishing achievements. He was made a Fellow of the Royal Society, and awarded their Gold Medal. He was also promoted to captain at last. But he had little time to enjoy his fame, for he volunteered to lead a further expedition into the Pacific to settle another age-old question—the North-West Passage.

Cook's second voyage. His ships were the first to sail round the world from west to east.

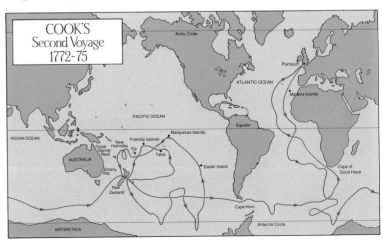

COOK'S
Second Voyage
1772-75

The fatal third voyage

For centuries—even before Magellan reached the Pacific—sailors had been searching for a way from the Atlantic to the Pacific by travelling north of the American continent. Their way had always been barred by the Arctic ice and by the hundreds of islands. But now that Cook had thoroughly explored the Pacific, it seemed natural to look for a passage from that side of the continent.

Cook's ship was once again the *Resolution*, and he was to be accompanied by the *Discovery*, another Whitby-built ship. They sailed separately in the summer of 1776 and met up at Cape Town. It soon became clear that the *Resolution* was in a very poor state—the hull leaked, and one of the topmasts was cracked—and throughout the voyage to come she had to be repaired frequently. But, after an extensive overhaul at Cape Town, both ships safely made their way to New Zealand and Tahiti—the last visit Cook was to make to this happy island. Carrying on northward, he discovered the Hawaiian (or Sandwich) Islands, and reached the west coast of North America, near the place which Francis Drake had named 'New Albion'.

It was then simply a matter of following the coast-line north and looking for a passage to the Atlantic. We now know that there is no passage, but the ships pushed on past Alaska and the Aleutian Islands, and into the Bering Sea—the small stretch of ocean between Siberia and Alaska. Eventually, they reached pack ice and were forced to turn back, hoping to try again the following summer.

By this time the hull and the rigging needed repairing, and Cook decided to spend the winter in the apparently friendly Hawaiian Islands. He landed on Hawaii itself, the largest island of the group (and one which he had not visited previously), and was amazed at the splendid reception he received. He did not know that the islanders believed him to be a god

Artists aboard Cook's ships frequently recorded the appearance and customs of the natives they met. This man is from the Hawaiian Islands.

The Resolution *and the* Discovery *in the Arctic ice.*

returning from the sea. They lavished their dwindling food and riches on Cook and his men, often going hungry themselves.

Death in Hawaii

Clearly, the Hawaiians must have been relieved when, in early February 1779, the two ships sailed away after a stay of three weeks. And they must have been greatly angered to see them returning a few days later. The *Resolution* had cracked a topmast in a storm, and Cook, reluctantly, was forced to turn back. This time, as he had feared, there was no welcome, and the natives began to steal from the ships. Then, on 14th February, it was discovered that the *Discovery*'s cutter (a small rowing boat) had been stolen. Cook decided that this theft was too important to be overlooked, and he landed with a party of marines to take the local chief hostage. A large crowd gathered and fighting broke out. Cook was unable to prevent his marines from opening fire, and, as he tried to get his men off the beach, he was savagely attacked and killed.

Once described as 'the most moderate, humane and gentle circumnavigator that ever went out upon discoveries', Cook had always been sensitive to the feelings of the natives he met, and it is especially tragic that his death was the result of an unhappy misunderstanding.

Cook's death in Hawaii.

Dates and events

Joshua Slocum

Slocum's early years at sea

Joshua Slocum was born into a pioneering family in Nova Scotia, Canada, in 1844. He grew up fast—he could handle a plough at the age of eight, and at ten he was set to work on his father's farm on Brier Island. But he hated the dull work of the farm, preferring to daydream about the sea, and whittle model ships from wood. Once, his father caught him idling and smashed a beautiful model he had just finished.

Joshua, still only twelve years old, decided that there was nothing for it but to run away to sea. The first time he tried he was caught and brought back, but he was soon off again, and managed to get a job as a cook on a fishing smack working in the Bay of Fundy. He knew immediately that this was the life for him, and, young as he was, he already dreamed of sailing around the world.

A born leader

It was not long before he travelled further afield. His first trip across the Atlantic was aboard a creaky old lumber carrier bound for Dublin. Here, Slocum left the ship and travelled across to Liverpool, then one of the major ports of the world. He was taken on by a British ship, and had his first sight of the Far East, visiting China, Manila and Singapore.

This is how the port of Liverpool looked at the time of Slocum's visit in the early 1860s.

At the age of eighteen, Joshua Slocum was already showing himself to be an outstanding seaman. He was big and strong, a born leader, and had mastered the art of steering a big ship. In his spare time he educated himself, not only learning navigation and astronomy, but reading widely in literature and history.

For the next twenty years he roamed the world as a trader, boat builder, ship's captain, fisherman and many other things. His first command, in 1869, was a schooner trading between Seattle and San Francisco on America's west coast. He spent the winter building a fishing boat and hunting for salmon in the Columbia River. Then, in 1870, he was made captain of another merchantman, the *Washington*, which was to sail to

The first ship that Slocum commanded was a schooner similar to this one.

A view of San Francisco from the bay, 1868.

Sydney, Australia, and return to fish for salmon in Alaska.

In Sydney, Slocum married an American girl, Virginia Walker, who was to share many of his adventures and who was to bear and bring up five children, mostly on board ship. Their honeymoon was spent in Cook Inlet, Alaska, where Joshua was to set up a fishing station for the valuable king salmon.

But the Inlet was a cold place, with perilous tides and icebergs. During a storm, the *Washington* was driven on to the beach, and the sand packed about her so tightly that she could not be shifted. Unflustered by this disaster, Slocum organized the building of a small whaleboat, in which he travelled to the nearest port and hired two schooners to carry the catch back to San Francisco.

With his growing family on board, Slocum now took command of the *Constitution*, sailing between San Francisco, Australia and the South Sea Islands. In the Southern Pacific he came across a bloodthirsty

buccaneer and slave-trader called Bully Hayes, who was posing as a missionary and wanted to buy a Bible from him! On the coast near Manila, he was hired to build a steamer—a difficult job, for there were scarcely any tools and no proper dock, and the workers were in danger every moment from crocodiles, scorpions and boa constrictors. But such hardships were a challenge to Captain Slocum, and the boat was launched successfully, being hauled into the sea by water buffaloes.

In 1881, he became joint owner of the *Northern Light*, a large clipper trading in the Atlantic and the Pacific. His second voyage in this was almost his last. Before the ship had even left New York harbour, a mutiny broke out in which the mate was stabbed to death. The murderer was taken off by the police, but threats of rebellion continued throughout the voyage. In Yokohama, Japan, another seaman tried to stab Slocum himself, only to be knocked to the ground. It was a relief when New York was once again in sight.

In 1881, Slocum became joint owner of this clipper, the Northern Light.

The voyage of the *Liberdade*

Back in New York, Slocum sold his stake in the *Northern Light* and became the sole owner of the smaller *Aquidneck*. His first voyage was carrying flour to Pernambuco in South America. During this journey, his wife died suddenly and was buried at Buenos Aires. After two more years of trading, Slocum married again, and, taking his new wife and his two sons with him—the youngest being only six years old—he set out on what was to be the *Aquidneck's* last voyage.

It was ill-fated from the first, for the ship soon began to leak in a hurricane. After taking various cargoes between Argentina and Brazil, the Captain was forced to employ some new seamen, many of whom were criminals. Thinking that there was money on board, these men plotted to kill the Slocums, but they were met by a hail of bullets which killed one and wounded another. On top of this, most of the crew, including Slocum, caught smallpox in Montevideo. Finally, after loading up with timber on the Brazilian coast early in 1888, the *Aquidneck* got stuck on a sandbank and was pounded to pieces by the waves.

Stranded

It seemed as though Slocum and his family were stranded thousands of miles from home. But the Captain had an astonishing plan. He started building a small boat which, once complete, would carry them all back to New York.

On 13th May, the boat was ready to be launched. She was built of timber from the wreck and from local cedar and ironwood trees, and the sails were sewn by Mrs Slocum. About 35 feet (10.7 metres) long and 7½ feet (2.3 metres) wide, she was named the *Liberdade*—the Spanish word for 'liberty'.

The boat was crammed with provisions and the Slocum family set out. It was soon clear that the *Liberdade* was a fine, well-balanced boat to sail, even in the roughest seas. On the first day, she covered 150 miles (240 kilometres). On the way to Rio de Janeiro, Slocum managed to get a tow from a steamer, which reached such a speed that the little ship was nearly swamped. Then they continued alone up the South American coast, often in danger, not only from storms, but also from whales, swordfish and reefs. One huge whale almost capsized them, and an iron bar had to be fitted to the hull to protect it from being cracked.

On and on they sailed, through tropical storms and silent moonlit seas. At night, flying fish would sometimes collide with the *Liberdade*'s sails and fall to the deck, providing a tasty meal the following day. When they reached Barbados, repairs were made and stores taken on board before the last stage of the remarkable voyage was begun. This soon took them into the Gulf Stream, which swept the *Liberdade* north at a great rate until they saw the coast of North America.

The Liberdade—*the boat which Slocum built to carry his family back from Brazil to New York.*

Flying fish would sometimes collide with the Liberdade's *sails and land on the deck, providing the Slocums with a tasty meal.*

A triumphant return

As they made their way up towards Washington, D.C., news of their voyage spread across the country, and, at the end of their amazing journey, they were famous. The *Liberdade* was eventually put on show in Washington.

Slocum's next adventure took him back to Brazil. Civil war had broken out there, and Slocum was hired to take a torpedo vessel to aid the government side. Called the *Destroyer,* she was a clumsy ship, very low in the water, with one huge torpedo gun 6½ feet (2 metres) below the waterline. She did not even have any spare room to carry her own fuel, and no company would take the risk of insuring the crew.

Somehow, Slocum managed to sail this monster to Bahia. She was towed through the rough seas by a large tug, and was often in danger of sinking, either because of leaks, or because of the sea washing over the sides. But, when Slocum arrived, the Brazilians took the *Destroyer* out of service and deliberately sank her, refusing to pay him and his crew. Slocum's anger was short-lived, however, for he was now planning the most daring exploit of his long career—a solo voyage around the world.

Alone against the oceans —Slocum's single-handed voyage

In 1892, Slocum was given the ruin of an old sloop —the *Spray*. He set about reconstructing her, plank by plank, with timber that he cut and cured himself. The result was an almost perfect craft, which would keep afloat in the foulest weather, and would remain on a set course even when the captain was not at the helm.

At long last, Slocum could fulfil his old ambition of sailing alone around the world. In 1895 he set out from Boston, Massachusetts. To stop himself feeling lonely, he began by shouting orders to an imaginary crew and then carrying them out himself! But it was not long before he got used to solitude—the *Spray* herself became his closest friend.

Chased by pirates

His first plan was to cross to the Mediterranean and sail through the Suez Canal to the Indian Ocean. But when he reached Gibraltar (after only a month's sailing) he was warned that he was likely to be attacked by pirates off the coast of North Africa. So he set off again across the Atlantic—and not a moment too soon, for he was chased by a fast pirate ship, and only escaped when his pursuers lost their sail in a squall.

With great relief he reached the Brazilian coast, passing on his way the wreck of the *Destroyer*. As he was approaching Montevideo, the *Spray* ran aground on a sandbank. When Slocum had secured the sloop with cables, he threw himself on to the sand to rest. He was woken by the sounds of a small boy on a horse, trying to tow the *Spray* and her rowing boat back to his village. Eventually, after making friends with the boy, Slocum was able to refloat his vessel and sail on to Montevideo, where he received a noisy welcome from all the ships at anchor, and was given a free refit.

Swamped by a tidal wave

His brushes with death continued. Before reaching the Straits of Magellan, the *Spray* was swamped by a

Slocum's boat, the Spray, *rebuilt from the ruin of an old sloop.*

The Spray *at anchor off Gibraltar.*

vast tidal wave. Slocum managed to scramble to safety up the mast, and he watched, horrified, as the deck of the boat disappeared below the foaming water. But the *Spray* stayed afloat, and on 11th February 1896 Slocum entered the Straits.

The local Indians were now used to seeing foreign boats, and they regularly attacked any strange craft in their war canoes. For a lone yachtsman, this was especially dangerous. But Slocum took prompt action as soon as a party of Indians approached, and fired his shotgun across their bows: the attackers quickly retreated. All the same, he was glad to be given a tow by a Chilean gunboat patrolling the Straits.

The *Spray* reached the Pacific on 3rd March, only to be met with a gale that drove her far to the south-west. Slocum found himself in the dreaded Milky Way, an

57

Slocum awoke to find a small boy trying to tow away the Spray's *rowing boat.*

The Spray *is swamped by a tidal wave.*

area of seething waters breaking over sunken rocks, where few vessels could survive for long. Only one other ship had been known to sail through it safely before the *Spray,* and Slocum described this part of the voyage as 'the greatest sea adventure of my life'. He reached the shelter of the mainland again, and headed back towards the Straits of Magellan.

Slocum's burglar alarm

He now had to make most of the passage again, and lay himself open to Indian attack. One night, as Slocum slept, the yacht was boarded by a group of robbers. As they clambered onto the *Spray,* they encountered the Captain's secret weapon—carpet-tacks scattered about the deck. Awoken by the howls of the barefooted Indians, Slocum appeared on deck and fired a few shots into the air—he was not disturbed again.

A brush with Indians in the Straits of Magellan.

Slocum leaving Melbourne, Australia.

On reaching the Pacific for the second time, he had better weather, and made his way across to Sydney, Australia, calling at Samoa on the way. He was given a splendid welcome in Sydney, and he boosted his flagging finances by giving a series of lectures about his voyage, all of which were packed out. After a pleasant rest and a trip to Melbourne, he turned north again, and by June 1897 was picking his way carefully through the Great Barrier Reef and into the Indian Ocean.

Sailing westward, he reached Mauritius on 19th September, and rounded the Cape of Good Hope and landed at Cape Town. Here, he gave more lectures, and travelled inland. He even met the President of the

Transvaal, Paul Kruger, who amused him greatly by insisting that the world was flat, even though Slocum had just sailed round it.

Dinner with the President

On 26th March 1898, he was homeward bound, and he finally reached his starting point, Fairhaven in Massachusetts, on 3rd July, amidst a storm of publicity—he had completed the first solo circumnavigation of the world. President Theodore Roosevelt later came aboard the *Spray*, and was cooked a fine dinner. Then, when Slocum published his account of the epic voyage, it became an immediate bestseller.

He retired at last, and bought himself a house on the island of Martha's Vineyard, where he combined a little sailing with a new-found passion for gardening.

In the autumn of 1909, the newly-refitted *Spray* set out once again from Rhode Island for South America. Neither the ship nor Slocum were ever seen again.

Joshua Slocum's single-handed voyage round the world.

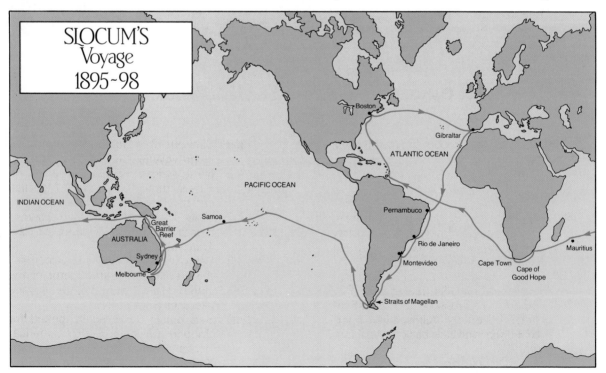

SLOCUM'S
Voyage
1895~98

Boston
Gibraltar
ATLANTIC OCEAN
PACIFIC OCEAN
INDIAN OCEAN
Samoa
Great
Barrier
Reef
AUSTRALIA
Sydney
Melbourne
Pernambuco
Rio de Janeiro
Montevideo
Cape Town
Cape of
Good Hope
Mauritius
Straits of Magellan

In 1909, Slocum set sail for the Orinoco River in South America. Both he and the Spray *disappeared without trace.*

Dates and events

1844   Joshua Slocum born in Nova Scotia, Canada.

1856   Runs away to sea.

1862   Sails to the Far East aboard British trading ship.

1869   Given his first command—a schooner trading on the west coast of America.

1881   Becomes joint owner of *Northern Light*, a large clipper.

1884   Sells *Northern Light* and buys *Aquidneck*, smaller trading boat.

1888   *Aquidneck* wrecked on coast of Brazil. Slocum builds new boat, *Liberdade*, and sails back to Washington, D.C.

1892   Begins rebuilding *Spray*.

1895   Sets out from Boston on round-the-world voyage. Chased by pirates off North African coast.

1896   Passes through Straits of Magellan and reaches Australia.

1897   Visits Mauritius and Cape Town—meets President Kruger of the Transvaal.

1898   Returns home to hero's welcome—the first solo circumnavigator of the world. His account of the voyage becomes a bestseller.

1909   Sets out in *Spray* again, bound for Orinoco River in South America. Neither Slocum nor *Spray* ever seen again.

Glossary

Assassinate   To kill someone treacherously, usually for political reasons.

Buccaneer   A pirate, especially one who attacked Spanish colonies and ships in the Caribbean.

Cannibal   A human being who eats human flesh.

Circumnavigate   To sail round something.

Collier   A ship designed to carry coal.

Financier   Someone who provides money for a scheme (an expedition, for example).

Fireship   A vessel which is loaded with explosives, ignited, and made to drift into an enemy's warships.

Monopoly   The sole right to make or sell something.

Moors   The Muslim people of North Africa, descended partly from the Arabs.

Mutiny   Rebellion against authority, especially by seamen or soldiers.

Press gang   A group of men employed to force civilians to join the navy or army.

Scurvy   A disease caused by a lack of vitamin C (fresh fruit and vegetables are rich in vitamin C).

Spanish Main   The north coast of South America, from where the Spanish shipped their gold and silver back to Spain.

Spice Islands   The old name for the Moluccas, a group of islands in the Far East where valuable spices were grown.

Strait   A narrow passage linking two large areas of sea.

'Terra Australis'   A huge, legendary continent which was believed to lie in the southern half of the world.

Yellow fever   A highly infectious tropical disease.

Further reading

Magellan
The First Ships Round the World by W. Brownlee (Cambridge University Press)
Ferdinand Magellan by Ruth Harley (Troll Associates)
Ferdinand Magellan: Noble Captain by Katherine Wilkie (Houghton-Mifflin)

Drake
Francis Drake by David Goodnough (Troll Associates)
Sea Dragon: The Journals of Francis Drake's Voyage Around the World by George Sanderlin (Harper and Row)

Cook
Captain Cook by Grove D. Day (Hogarth Press)
Captain James Cook by Bill Harley (Troll Associates)

Captain Cook and the South Pacific by Oliver Warner and J. C. Beaglehole (American Heritage)
The Story of Captain Cook by L. Dugarde Peach and John Kenney (Merry Thoughts)

Slocum
Sailing Alone Around the World by Joshua Slocum (Sheridan House Inc.)
Captain Joshua Slocum: The Life and Voyages of America's Best Known Sailor by Victor Slocum (Sheridan House Inc.)
In the Wake of the Spray by Kenneth E. Slack (Sheridan House Inc.)
First to Sail the World Alone: Joshua Slocum by Jan Fortman

Index

Picture acknowledgements

The publisher would like to thank all those who provided illustrations on the following pages: E. T. Archive 31 (bottom); Mary Evans Picture Library 20, 28 (top), 29 (bottom), 41 (bottom), 47, 50, 51 (top), 61; BBC Hulton Picture Library 8, 15 (top), 18 (top), 19, 25, 31 (top), 33, 36, 37; Mansell Collection 6 (top), 13, 16, 40 (bottom), 57 (bottom), 58 (top), 59 (top and bottom); National Maritime Museum, Greenwich 23, 32 (top), 41 (top), 43; National Maritime Museum, Greenwich/Photo Michael Holford *front cover*, 11, 34, 46 (bottom); Smithsonian Institution, Washington, D.C. 54; Malcolm S. Walker 4, 12, 17, 29 (top), 44 (bottom), 48, 52, 57 (top), 58, 60. The remaining pictures are from the Wayland Picture Library.